kyrie

kyrie

BARBARA COLEBROOK PEACE

Sono
Nis
Press

VICTORIA • BRITISH COLUMBIA

National Library of Canada Cataloguing in Publication Data

Peace, Barbara Colebrook
      Kyrie

      Poems
      ISBN 1-55039-117-8

      I. Title.
PS8581.E2K97 2001   C811'.54 C2001-910078-7
PR9199.3.P38K97 2001

Sono Nis Press gratefully acknowledges the support of the Canada Council for the Arts and the Province of British Columbia, through the British Columbia Arts Council.

Edited by Linda Rogers
Copy edited by Dawn Loewen
Cover painting, *Renewal*, by Heather Keenan
Cover and interior design by Jim Brennan

Published by
Sono Nis Press
PO Box 5550, Stn. B
Victoria, BC V8R 6S4
tel: (250) 598-7807
sono.nis@islandnet.com
www.islandnet.com/sononis/

Printed and bound in Canada by Morriss Printing Company Ltd.

The Canada Council | Le Conseil des Arts
for the Arts | du Canada

ACKNOWLEDGEMENTS

Thanks to my husband, Terry Peace, without whose loving support this book could not have been written. *Kyrie* is his as much as it is mine.

Linda Rogers edited the manuscript with characteristic grace and generosity, encouraged me to go further, and always understood.

Kelly Parsons has been a companion on this book's journey from first to last. She, more than anyone, taught me by her example "a choreography of the waiting."

"Blessed are the merciful." Barbara Youds taught me about mercy.

Rona Murray gave very generously of her time, energy, and enthusiasm to introduce six new women poets, of whom I was one, in *Threshold: Six Women, Six Poets* (Sono Nis Press, 1998).

Many thanks also to Rhonda Batchelor for publishing my chapbook *Twelve Silences* (Reference West, 1998), and to Linda Rogers for selecting my work for the anthology *Breaking the Surface* (Sono Nis Press, 2000).

I am grateful to Dorothy Field, Connie Frey, Don McKay, Rona Murray, Susan Stenson, Barbara Youds and Patricia Young for their insightful comments and suggestions.

I would like to thank the editors of the following journals, in which some of these poems first appeared: *The Antigonish Review, Arc, The Fiddlehead, The Malahat Review,* and *Vintage 93* (League of Canadian Poets).

Many thanks to Sono Nis Press: Diane Morriss, who has worked extraordinarily hard to keep a small press alive and give new writers publication; Heather Keenan, inspired artist, whose beautiful painting I'm honoured to have on the cover of this book; Dawn Loewen, copy editor *ne plus ultra;* and Jim Brennan, outstanding designer.

Family and friends have been wonderfully supportive. I would specially like to thank Marga von Rudloff and Otto Peace.

Thanks to the B.C. Arts Council for a grant in the year 2000 which enabled me to complete this manuscript.

Finally, I would like to thank P.K. Page for the inspiration of her life in poetry: "Distilled from all this living, / all this gold."

I sing in the shadow of your wings

— Psalm 63 verse 7

contents

entries of birds

shadow icarus

When he was a boy, he spent hours
flat on his stomach on the floor, drawing
cartoons of trucks, remembering not to
crayon over the lines. His mother
moving somewhere about the house—
the passage of the sun across the sky.

Now he lives alone. He looks
for a moment at the rain, stretches
his feet to warmth by the heater.
So many years caring for his mother
since his father left; and then her death —

> Again he hears a bang
> against the glass, observes
> the near wing raised, far wing
> stilled, feathers lightly stirring.

He takes from the table the leather-bound
journal *On the Flight of Birds*,
he's kept for sixty years. Writes
sandpiper, and pauses. Each night
he dreams of stars, water, trees;
a lost limbshadow aches behind his shoulder.
Everything that was perfect, he holds
between wind-remembering wings:
his mother's voice calling, and the careful
entries of birds.

The Gargoyle

Who was it left him here,
stuck between Coca-Cola and Christ?
When ice chunks him, sometimes he forgets
whether he's a curlicued bladder of frost
or a guttered stammer of stone.

But he remembers summer: dust-pregnant,
bibilical yellow. Pilgrims chanting, winding
through the streets; his thick tongue
hanging mottled and slack,
while the cathedral clock
ticks through hot grunge, till
dusk turns him into a battered psalm.

*

The pigeons' skinny feet
dicker over snow. He watches
all the apocalyptic signs of the sky.
Cherubim and seraphim
dart through the steeple's amethyst eye,
too cold to babble amens.

Who was it left him here,
with lacerated wings? Wind
shakes him in epileptic fits.
When traffic baffles him with fumes,

sometimes he forgets
whether he's a limb of the enemy,
a sad cloth of ashes,
or the mercies of never —

*

His mouth startles O-pen
wide enough to swallow God's kingdom:

— no, he's forgotten
what he meant to ask.

Something about slums, a lurch, a slurred star?
Something about a wounded door?

He would lick the cobbled street
if only he could find the right prayer.

Kyrie for a sleeping Mother

When I heard they hadn't got all the cancer,
I could have hurled a brick at God
and watched it mash his nose to pulp.

*

Should I wake her for lunch, or let her sleep?
The shepherd's pie is done.
I stand in the doorway like a small child
at the edge of the sea. They have taken away
most of her upper lip.
A line of black stitches makes tottery
crosses underneath her nose,
a sleeping field of losses.

There has been a movement in the earth's crust.
She's an exposed rock face
where miners tap and hammer.
She's the witch's chin, mouth, eyes, nose,
forehead, I used to see in the cracks
of the lavatory wall. The muscles in her face
twitch, tighten and relax. *Why did they
make me look so cross?* she said this morning. *Don't
let the children come to see me.*

*

She loved to buy her slips, peach,
ivory, beige, from Fenwick's French;
Mind you, I always get them in the sales.
Now she wears slacks because they're easier.
Too tired to undress, she lies
on top of the bedspread
in green trousers, white blouse, powder blue cardi.
The nurses, she told me, loved the crimson
bra and panties she bought for hospital.

*

What happened to the white smocks
with crimson cross stitches she made
for my sister and me? Did she later
give them away? The little girls
who wore those smocks sleep
somewhere in a photo album. After
we were at last in bed, she tucked
her anxiety away
in a closet with a creaking door. Her face
in those old photos dreamy, lips
parted over slightly crooked teeth.

*

Ride a white horse to Banbury Cross.
When she was a child, the furthest away
was a day trip to Stanhope;
feeling a bit sick on the school bus,
then leaping across the stepping stones
that ford the river Wear. There are
no photos of the child she was, wearing
her elder sisters' clothes
handed down with careful stitches, her skin
soft as pussy willow, when she first learned
to tell time on a clock face,
add two apples to four, and then
take one away.

in this small room

(i)

the sun sits tight on my back.
they are making a mask
for my mother's face

two nurses
move her head, gently

       try to relax, breathe
            normally

they hoist the table up, joke
they will take her for a ride
their movements small ceremonies
they place a stocking on her face

       you'll make me into
          a burglar

I watch: now a third of her
upper lip is gone; her mouth
silently flutters,
the cage of her chest swells

inside there is
a small bird

      stunned.

(ii)

I wait outside her sleep.

they must place her face,
line it up precisely.
two move her head,
one checks alignments
of morning / afternoon.

often my mother asks me
is it wednesday today?

I can count
holding a buttercup
under her chin:
thirty days hath september,
april, june and   I count
her feet
in yellow socks
important as sparrows.

(iii)

sitting in her chintz-flowered armchair
she spoons in chocolate mousse
from marks and spencers
with a baby-size plastic spoon
through the small opening of her mouth.

she sets her cup of tea down
till it's cool enough to drink
through a straw; but her mouth
is too sore; later,
I will pour it down the sink.

I want another language,
neither mother nor daughter,
to praise her

wickaninnish   ("Place of Roaring Waters")

(i)

Now you are here. Where the first people
saw the world arrive in flickering
interstices of rain, the mountains
and trees shaping themselves
at the edge of the sky, the colours
free-floating, turning
after rain. And in the later
silence, not yet knowing what they
left behind, they woke;
listened to the pebbled dark.

You are here, the sign says, but
you want to be before that, you want
to stand wide and cedared in the sun,
the swift clusters of hail,
the songs of a bird
opening silence —

(ii)

the beach is beyond purpose.

she walks eggshell fine
in the rain; leaves behind

unnecessary kindness. she sits
by the dark window

looking at the sea. observes
the sad side of nothing.

she wakes in the night
hearing the rain

stop. she has lost
the turquoise map,

the exact times of the rising
and setting of the sun.

the measures of her life,
small brown birds

fly from her hands

no is where

Yes, they've had their nostrils blocked up with wax, they get home. They've had confusing smells like turpentine put on their beaks, they get home. And just in case that doesn't work, they've had their olfactory nerves severed. . . . Whereas all previous experiments involved moving the pigeons from their home, my experiments involve moving the home from the pigeons.

—Rupert Sheldrake

Woozy, in a world of constant warm,
we sit woolgathering, wings against
our dozy sides. Cubicled in fluorescent summer,
our breathing dims to autumn mould.
Though we don't know the reason,
in our brains, the cherry trees are leaking.

We've never known anything but here:
white sloping chute, white floor,
a legend of a door that leads to starlight.
We sit, are sitting, sat, have sat, will sit.
The white-coated ones watch over us,

show us slides from time to time
of senseless green. We've learned
which dots to peck to get our grain,
which ones clang a shock
throughout our cells. We haven't figured
what they want from us, unless
they're lost and hope for some idea

of how they could get home —
but we can't think about it. Not
over breakfast. Later, after lunch,
we tell ourselves that if and if and if
the letter comes,
and we are free once more,
we'll stumble over somehow to the door,
folding our hearts in grace

Reading in a Nursing Home

One day perhaps we'll be glad to remember even these things.

—Virgil, *Aeneid*

Snow is falling absently, as though it had
forgotten
any other way of being water. I hang
my hat and coat in the hall, enter
the Activity Room, where some residents
are sitting, while others
are wheeled in. Each windowsill now
has its quota of snow, wafer thin,
rationed like butter in the war.

Inside, the thermostat is set at seventy-two.
It's snowing, we tell each other and rest
in words known all our lives. *It's
snowing:* I hear the words echo back
to snowmen we built as children. How they lost
parts of themselves
before they disappeared.

Here they sit, who once wore high heels and hats
trimmed with cherries or black veils,
the men in braces and starched shirts.
I begin to read. Some residents join in,
a little lag between the words:

'Twas the night before… Christmas,
and all through the…house —
I'm reading now for all who mourn
the mother who read to us long ago.

Tore open the shutters and threw up the sash.
The moon on the breast of the new-fallen snow —

I'm sitting beside my mother to watch
the first men walk on the moon:
the long cool floating toward joy.
"That this should happen
in our lifetime!" she says.
Someone steps on the moon and in that pause
I see again my mother's face,
as it was before and after
surgery. Brave

as an astronaut, she
looked after my sister, father, brother,
when each had cancer,
and shortly before she died,
attended my brother's wedding,
a wide-brimmed hat and make-up protecting from the sun
her face, where part
was gone.

Now, Dasher! now, Dancer! now, Prancer and Vixen!
On, Comet!, on Cupid! on, Donner and Blitzen!

Five years since she died. Standing here
to read, while snow
falls thicker on the windowsill,
I see her clearly:
the ribboned hat, scarred nose, thinned upper lip.
Her face still puffy
from surgery and radiotherapy.
Her make-up glossy from the heat.
She's sitting in a lawn chair with raised glass,
bright dress, red shoes; I think
we're about to drink a toast.

He sprang to his sleigh, to his team gave a whistle.
And away they all flew —

The poem ends. The residents
applaud, break into chatter, while Theresa
brings round cups of tea.
Our memories are astronauts, floating
each toward another moon.
Those who listen are there too:

it's snowing now in distant constellations.

songs of Mary: how could I know?

The first time in my life I saw snow
I was a child, running home from the field.
How could I know what I'd seen?
How could I say what it was?

I was a child, running home from the field.
I let the flakes land on my tongue.
How could I say what it was?
The day the angel came and I said Yes,

I tasted a new song on my tongue;
I wanted to run and dance and shout.
The day the angel came and I said Yes,
How could I know what Yes would mean?

I wanted to run and dance and shout!
The apricot sky seemed full of wings.
How could I know what Yes would mean?
From the roof I watched houses move into dark;

The apricot sky was full of wings.
A goat bleated, and fell silent.
I watched from the roof. Houses moved into dark,
the ram's horn sounded for sabbath.

A goat bleated, and fell silent.
I looked at the darkening hills and sky.

The ram's horn sounded for sabbath.
I thought of thousands of children not yet born —

I looked at the darkening hills and sky.
How could I know what I'd seen?
I thought of thousands of children not yet born,
and the first time in my life I saw snow.

The white cliffs of Dover

There'll be blue birds over the white cliffs of Dover
Tomorrow, just you wait and see.
There'll be love and laughter and peace ever after
Tomorrow, when the world is free.

—Nat Burton, 1941

You always ask for number seven in the songbook.
Usually you're spry and alert, but today
your neck droops like a poppy
after rain, as if your remembrance
were pinned to the lapel of a long-lost
gaberdine. You told me once: *I'm clever*
at getting lost. Yet when I play
an opening chord on the piano,
somehow with the music you recover
There'll be blue birds over the white cliffs of Dover

along with the smell of the earth in Devonshire
where you were born, the schoolboy address
you printed in your Latin primer
ending with THE WORLD, the wail of an air raid
siren, gas and gunfire, and your first
taste of an orange after the war. Only
last week you recited
some lines from "The Owl and The Pussycat"
along with me; you can still sing
Tomorrow, just you wait and see,

and mean it — even though tomorrow
will be much like today. You'll have lunch
at a table set for four, each person's place
flagged with their name. There'll be
soft mashed potato and gravy, stewed
apples and custard. There'll be banter
with your neighbour; you'll put on
a broad Scottish accent or Cockney.
But the tide is slowly coming in. When we offer
There'll be love and laughter and peace ever after

our voices swirl and fuddle,
foam against white cliffs, the blue
varicose veins of your calves.
In the years I've been visiting
here once a week,
you've told me only part of a story.
What will you tell me in another
tomorrow, when the moat
round your heart fills with the sea?
Tomorrow, when the world is free.

small
moon

Beginnings

In the beginning, I wanted
to drink the sky.

What could it matter, a woman
feeding hens, a workman
with his ladder against a roof?
Mountains crouched under my wrist.

The sea was white and milky where I fell.

Here, where the stars are heard more
deeply, centuries of plankton
fall through silence, cool
my burning mouth, settle
in small crevices of my wings.

   Bones drift together and apart.

Tentative, I begin
      as dissolved light
filters through the hole where once
a shoulder was, gaps
      in my salt-caked thumbs.

Sometimes I dream of hand or foot,
the way I caught light
under my wings.

Nameless ones
nestle in my limbs: sea-purple,
ivory, dim gold.

Someday I will be a new
land.

Inuit sculpture: *Woman,* by Lucy Kanayok

Silent in her parka, her smooth head
is tilted up to listen, not speak.

The wide silence of her shoulders
self-contained; her feet
breakable, tiny strength and immensity.

She's looking at the far side
of the moon, where it's always
dark to earth:

beyond the deliberate
footprint, the four-leaf clover
and the falcon feather   ——

             illumination
         composed and abandoned,
                ultima Thule.

Epitaph for a Gargoyle

He died before men walked on the moon.

He had a face once; perhaps an old faun
or an eagle, or a sleeping angel, turned
into the shelter of wings. Now
wind and rain have bitten him
down to an eyeless core.
Only his arms are left to glare,

when thawed icicles
drip from the ledge above,
and his gouged belly grieves
for someone
       only snow remembers.
Grief follows the furrows of his wings,
echoes inside him as a hollow slush.

When he sleeps, illegible
plums appear; night
presses on him star by star,
and scudding clouds
sweep chimneys into darkness —

Then his knees loosen
and fingers slacken; leaving the grass
unmown, the Scrabble board paused,
like the Rosetta stone, for us to decipher

a word that might be *swort* or *startle* ——

How could we know he was our father?

small moon

and swan dives. I think each memory is lit
by its own small moon — a snowberry,
a mothball, a dime — which regulates its tides
and longings. Next time I am going to lift the oars
   — Don McKay, "Finger Pointing at the Moon"

November. On the beach at Wickaninnish, I watch a beetle
make its way in fits and starts, dot dot
dash, leaving a track of furrowed sand: memory,
until the tide comes in. When my father died, my mother
put away all photos, never spoke his name, walked out
of the room when someone on TV sang "Moonlight
Becomes You." This morning, sleet thickened into hailstones,
hammering the sand with such force they made small
wounds. Sometimes the memory gets hurt, takes fright
and swan dives. I think each memory is lit

and darkened and lit again as these rocks
and tide pools are submerged and rediscovered,
a sand dollar breathing,
a starfish drifting from one end of a pool
to the other. Here's another beetle, meandering
toward some logs. Does it know its own starry
heaven? Constellations of frost on driftwood,
comets of hailstones? And the memory, when it slips
through the night, lit obscurely
by its own small moon — a snowberry,

perhaps, blown here by a storm — how could it conceive
the waves between here and Japan? I climb cedar
stairs to the restaurant and museum, thinking
of my father, how he never got to come here.
Ghosts of summer children lick ice cream. Grief,
which is always listening to the ocean, sometimes
finds itself in smaller waters,
fishing in a rowboat for a sunken moon —
a frosted marble, an ammonite,
a mothball, a dime — which regulates its tides

and the rhythm of its curled-up hours.
I hold a seashell to my ear, and listen
to the stones in a river, where a child
paddles with her father, a jam-jar set in the rocks
to hold minnows they will afterwards let go;
the lapping of a city pond, where they explore
a half moon that bends into reedbeds and swans, the mother
waving from the shore. The father rows, the child
sits in the stern. She was too small then for her desires
and longings. Next time I am going to lift the oars

gobs

Whisht! lads, haad your gobs,
and I'll tell ye aal an aaful story
Whisht! lads, haad your gobs,
and I'll tell ye 'boot the Worm

—"The Lambton Worm," song from northeast England

There are too many people in the world
I'm thinking as I get off the bus
at the corner of Douglas and Yates.
And you're right here, sitting
on the sidewalk, staking your claim
to the niche between trashcan and doorway.
Holes in the knees of your jeans,
rings in ear and nose, your cap
salted with a few quarters. *Spare*
some change for one good joke?

I hurry away without offering
a dime, but you follow me
that night into a dream, standing
just outside the bedroom door
on the upstairs landing of my childhood.
Who are you? I ask, dropping
to the bottom of a shaft. You say
nothing. *What do you have to give me?*
You spit:

      a gob

*

I swallow, eyes closed, and I'm back:

Shut your gob
   Ha'way man
      Why aye man
Where're ye gangin', hinny?

swirl down back streets and alleys
where we stir fresh tar in the gutter
with lollipop sticks, making treacle
    rainbows

Mrs. Keenan at the kitchen sink
swishing bacon grease from an iron
frying pan, tells me
Miners never wash their backs, pet.
    Mr. Keenan,
back drenched with soot, descends
in a cage to the bottom of the world,
hunkers with a shovel in the pit.
His spine knobbed with scars
scrapes against the ceiling
as he crabs backward on all fours
to his cold tea, bread and bacon dripping.
In a corner, a pit pony, sooty withers,
going blind, sniffs air breathed in and out
a thousand times.
    Far above their heads

Cheviot sheep straggle along Hadrian's Wall,
where slaves of Roman villas once
fetched coal, and soldiers glinted
against the wind's howl

*

The triangle of grass across the road
is my wilderness.
I clamber over iron railings.
I'm a wild horse, silver brumby,
mane and tail streaming in the wind,
whickering and neighing, hooves pounding

*

Green water at the reservoir
reflects trees and hills, and our uncle
puffing on his pipe. He tells us
it was near here
he and some other village boys
stalked through waist-high heather,
beating grouse for gentlemen to shoot.
A young lord looks down from his horse, asks
Are ye thirsty, lads?
Aye, they mutter, and he answers
Suck on a pebble

*

We play Sardines with our cousins,
cram ourselves in closets,
swish against lavender in wardrobe,
squeeze down a passageway,
crouch in the cubbyhole, sucking
in our breath, jam-packed small as possible
foot against foot
        elbow to elbow
clutching our giggles, sticky
as candy floss,
till there is only one of us seeking—

I always want to be found.
Don't let me be
the only one left in a gobsmacked
speechless world

        ****

We flew over mountains
vast as childhood coming here.
We could see clear back
to the world's spacious beginning:
        earth just risen from the sea
and all doors open

        *

Since you came to me, dream
figure, street person, outcast,
I know I need to eat
the seed words of my first home:
She's a canny bairn . . .

I think of my unborn children
and of the wildflowers
we found sprawling everywhere
along the wooden railroad and down by the river
near my mother's village.
We chose one of each, unwrinkled
their petals,
pressed them under white tissue,
wanting to fix them perfect forever:
cowslip, bluebell, primrose.

*

I walk down Fort Street past
the Dutch Bakery, pies in the window
decorated with gobs of whipped cream.

Buses come and go with gasping doors.
  Are ye thirsty, lads?

Spare some change for one good joke.
You're not here today. What joke
would you have told me?

Something sits unswallowed
like a stone in my mouth. *Gobstoppers*,
we used to call those sweets:
      bulging
          globes
we moved from cheek to cheek. Wodges
      so huge

we couldn't speak around them.

Icarus at Knossos

My father stitching feathers
was a great owl hunched in silence.
Every now and then he stood and stretched,
confirmed the position of the sun,
told me we would soon be going home.

Home, I said, falling
from sleep into sleep into water green as cucumber:
sun slants on the wood of my bed and stool,
my little statue of Heracles.
My sister crying over a wooden doll,
blotched with ancient rain.

I run home through the dark
with the wingspan of a falcon,
the Acropolis
far and tiny as the murmur
thalassa, thalassa of the sea.

My mother's voice dwindles into a moth,
the whirl of my knucklebones
as I play jacks on the floor.
Another voice, more ancient,
holds me in the black folds of her lap;
sings in the Lydian mode
a lullaby for dragonflies and kings.

songs of mary: i can't pray

I can't pray. I can only say *Please*.
Check first: he's not on the roof.
Look everywhere down the street and back.
Search behind the well and round the marketplace.

Check again. Still not on the roof.
Smacked him and the next time I looked, he was gone.
I ask everyone at the well and in the marketplace.
No one has seen him, no one knows.

Smacked him. Next time I looked, he was gone.
What about the cave where he sometimes plays?
No one has seen him, no one knows.
Heart clatters running up the hill.

It's dark in the cave where he sometimes plays.
I sweat. My stomach aches with longing.
Heart clatters running back down the hill.
Please I stumble, *please please*. Fall.

I sweat. My stomach aches with longing.
Oops-a-daisy, what I say to him
when *please* he stumbles, all fall down.
Fingers against mouth smell of onions.

Oops-a-daisy, what I say to him.
Sometimes I have to tell him *No*.

Fingers against mouth smell of onions.
I'll do anything if *please* he can be found.

Was I wrong when I told him *No?*
I look everywhere down the street and back.
Anything if *please* he can be found.
I can't pray. I can only say *Please*.

Learning Aramaic

More angels come to teach him
the stuttering of pain
till he can pronounce it three times out of ten.

His tongue repeats the syllables of light:
     soon   *morning*   *late*
He makes them lie shut around his heart.

He folds his mother's dreams
under the sleek wisdom of his lungs,
and in the dark cavities of knees.

She takes him to the rooftop and he swoops
     over gangling air; his arms
         begin their vertigo —-

      His father rocks him
         in clouds of Aramaic.

Rain enters through his smallest bones.

Each cell,
the multitude of branching passages and veins

listens

The visitor

Glorious it is to see
The caribou flocking down from the forests
And beginning
Their wandering . . .

—Netsik, Canadian Inuit

The gallery is warm. No breath of wind.
Three perfumed ladies
leave their scent behind, move on.

On the brown carpet
the visitor stands alone
to one side: a woman of uncertain age
holding a child. Her hands
are carelessly
supportive; seemingly, her thoughts
are elsewhere.

The paintings on the walls
the shapes of the sculptures
don't interest her. What she sees
is snow:

      newly drifted

      first snow

      spreading snow

      drifting

      beating snow

salty snow
watery snow
drinkable
building snow

In her language there are twenty-three
words for snow.

She has travelled a long way to this
temperature-and-humidity-controlled
gallery.

Now she stands staring
far across the snow
at the caribou flocking over the land:

Hush now.
Listen . . . snow

Deer, Fort Rodd

Yesterday we saw their absence,
lifting shadowed heads
cool in the wind of their startle
as we walked up the hillside,
the grass half empty, the seagulls
quiet and few.

When we came to the black
steel cannon pointing
smartly at the past, we stood
following its finger, as though
there might be something to see
out in the deep ocean —

We moved away, turned
to the daffodils
along the old brick wall.
Something had chosen
not to be spoken; the wind
had bitten its tongue.

old donkey, scarborough beach

Sometimes trying to remember
begets only forests of anonymous darkness
where the crowd pushes and shoves against a rope,
and the ritardando of the ice-cream van
clots your hide with flies, doodling
the same tune over and over,

while you, ignoring sharp pulls on the reins,
shrill cries of frisbee and football,
plod sturdily on.
You know, better than the blue-jeaned
girl who walks beside you, the exact
inch where you must turn;
where you begin, and stop. Almost anything else

is irrelevant. Yet there are gaps,
a *hush* and *hush* and *hush*
through which a no man's land appears.
Your maps peter out abruptly at the edge,
open into the void a long way down —

I would like to take you to a moon
and rinse
the crannies of your splotched ears and muzzle,
and give you water to drink
so slowly and gently that you'd remember
what you knew before:
the way to the grass beyond the sand dunes —

where in the luminous haze
all eternity has passed, and you
would glimmer over the dust
and stubble of another earth.

North
of
sorrow

Before the Rain was Born

Before the rain was born,
did you turn and stare
at the glimmer of a double helix form
caught in a web of sun? Or when

you closed the dark fastenings
of the moon, and flung the first
quark in a backwards
silver curve — was it then

you found a spiral shape in the dust,
scrabbling like a bird limed
in a net? While angels
swooped round the logic of the sun —

you pitched a stone deep into the dark,
so that you could dream

      the orbit of a human breath

Twenty Questions

'Twas brillig, and the slithy toves . . .
          — Lewis Carroll, "Jabberwocky"

What is a slithy tove? you ask me
when we meet in the corridor
on the way to poet's corner and the singsong:
a sign you remember who I am,
though my name has drifted like the sun
behind a cloud. Neither of us has a compass,

but we walk more or less north of sorrow
toward the Activity Room,
the question billowing round you
like a too big macintosh on a windy day.
I watch you find your way
through the dark intervals in your brain

to a chair beside someone you recognise;
you've told me several times she's
not your wife. You squelch across the room
through rain and wind-blown clouds,
clasping the word *home* so you won't fall.
Everything is just out of your reach:

though you would like to touch
the name and address your father

inked inside every item of stiff
new uniform, satchel and Latin grammar.
Syllable by syllable, we climb
out of your sight
on rungs of invisible riddles,
hic haec hoc over the gym horse,
amo amas amat, returning to a home
that is always more remote.

Now your clothes are labelled for the
laundry, taken and delivered by a stranger.
You stoop over an artificial flower;
doubt falls around you like soot.
What is Saturday afternoon?
Your wife died of cancer. Now there's
a chair, a piano, a woman you sit beside
in an animal, vegetable, mineral / mourning.

What is a slithy tove? you ask again
when I've finished reading poems,
"Daffodils," "The Cremation of Sam McGee,"
Lewis Carroll, Edward Lear,
and sit beside you while you drink your tea.
I don't know, I say. *What do you think?*

Maybe you were once
a great flanking buttress of stone,
a lover, a father, a maverick, a moon,
a face that slid round a corner, playing
hide and seek; someone

who made for your children
a shadow rabbit, one long ear pricked
against the dark.

grandfather

When he asked us to imagine swans,
winter-dreaming swans
flew through the long halls of another earth;
snow leopards returned
soft-footed to the mountains.

When he began the wrath
of the ponderosa tiger, and the love of S'ung
for the Moon's third daughter, his hands
made moonlight over ancient canyons,
covered oak and arbutus with hosannas of snow.

For the world began with snow, when the violet
leopard roared upon the mountain . . .

The long ago rainforest
echoed the *brek-kek-kek* of web-footed frogs.
His fingers made waves
for the dark curve of dolphin,
blue of camas and red of cedar,
the golden-winged corrugated cotton
phonograph . . .

Once upon a time there was a peacock —

O when it sang, it shivered
with a thousand turquoise eyes.

Then we danced the cougar
as we crossed the savanna, ravenous
to feast on orange mushrooms,
mahogany apples.

Show us the elephant again.
  How big was an oak?

He made rivers of scarlet finch, mountains
that gonged with the tongue of the cobra, whirring
hoopoe tigers, waterfalls of hawk.
At last the emerald towers
froze solid in the iceberg heave of Ocean.
Yet in the coffins of his eyes
white-gold anemones
                    held summer stemmed.

chinese embroidery

#E907. Exquisitely worked in satin stitch and the famous Peking stitch, interspersed with gold couchwork . . .

Thin as a rose in winter
under her section of window, she sits
straight. Sometimes she sings an old song
loudly to herself (the ballad
in which the young wife dies
is her favourite); sometimes she laughs
when one of the other women
says something she can't hear.

Now she is nearly seventy, everyone
calls her "Auntie." Her fine-boned fingers
support pillars of royal pavilions,
confirm within these borders
all the abundant life she imagines:

Butterflies skim in pairs, silver carp
gleam like thoughts in the imperial waters
under the red, childish orb of sun.
                Prince and princess
pause on a delicate bridge,
unfinished between branches of willow.
When did they begin, in her small hands?

Already she has given them
their tiny seed stitch mouths.
From the beginning, she has known
the end. Their hands
will seize the sun, will trade
her children's children
for the brief spice of cinnamon,
and a fine-wrought
earring of lavender jade.

She threads her needle with gold
for dragonfly wing; turns
to prince and princess, poised
on the arc of the bridge. Today
she'll add their eyes.

icarus in old age

From the palace rooms above, laughter
and the sound of a flute. It's always
cool down here, and I don't mind the stale
air or the spiders, the stone floor chill
under my bare feet. This is the safe
place I visit every day, a storage room where
no one ever comes. The wings

wait for me here, unspoiled and beautiful,
deep in the cedar chest — too small for me
now. You can still see where they once
fitted my vertebrae. How they
tickled when my father held them against
my spine, muttering over measurements, high
in the labyrinth tower. The first time I had them on,
I stretched my arms and swished

awkwardly round the room, uncertain
as a fledgling heron. Later, growing bolder,
I ran and swooped, making hullabaloo
until my father swore *Enough, by Zeus!*
and made me take them off (*Carefully,
carefully, or you'll damage the feathers.*)

The day he chose for our escape, I squatted
on the ledge. Looking down, I could see
the palace, the House of the Axe,

and the labyrinth far below, small as
ivory carvings; specks of fishing boats
far out to sea, bobbing up and down —

Nausea filled my belly.
I was dizzy as the day we climbed
Mount Ida, when my father's calloused
hands grabbed me as I fainted.
                                    I saw him once
take an axe and cleave right through the wood,
splitting it for one of his sculptures.
So it was with me. I watched another Icarus
fly off exultant, leaving me behind.
        Don't fly too near the sun!
My father shouted, but already my brother
was too far to hear. And my father, cursing,
flew off after him —

After that, whenever I tried to write
the words *son* and *father*, hearing my father's
voice from far away, I dropped
sullen letters
backwards in the wax. I was a lamb
stuck in a ewe the wrong way
round, unable to be born. Cautiously
I lived, counting each year to seventy-one.

Daedalus is long gone, my mother too. Upstairs,
the flautist begins a new song. I gather
the wings, smelling of cedar, in my arms,

carry them along the corridor, and out
to the tower my father built, stone
discoloured now with age. A breeze
is blowing inland from the sea; I climb
some stairs and rest, and climb again.

After last night's storm,
morning wraps the world in frail bandages;
defiant light slips through clouds.
The sun slowly forms
some letters bigger and rounder,
a tentative iota, then
the perfect shape of an omega —

I hold the wings against my cheek.
Their familiar fragrance comforts me.
Will it be a second chance, at last
a birth, dropping the umbilical of fear
beneath me on the sea?
                My self
leaving home for the first time
in a whistle of disappearing darkness;
the letters of my name
            in loops and whorls
that change with the colours of the sky.

not even solomon

for Tusen Tack, our stray cat

You came to us a question,
expecting the answer No.

Now you're sitting on my desk in the sun,
and not even Solomon

in all his glory
had such a rich chocolate underbelly.

At the snowflakes, first of the year, you
yatter as you do at crows:

What fables of snow do you imagine?
How far is it to the end of snow?

You want to hunt the snow
and so do I. Let's sign a treaty:

If you will have pity on my six words
as they scuttle round the room,

I promise I will wait here till my ears
are translucent as yours;

till I can discern
the flinch of a sparrow bone.

schrodinger's cat

At night I assume the windowsill.

I have counted the grey stars
   riveted in the co-eternal lid,
and the distance to the sides.

      Wherever the sun
strokes my half-silvered, elongated tail,
            I ambulate
      between tall possibilities

Wherever a rose
         is
a crimson probability,
            I cause striped coolness
   in the spaces between shadows.

      I stalk
the rustle of stars,
         approaching with my thought
   the pathway where the moon   may finally

                              emerge.

While you are waiting,
   sleeping in singular silence,
and learning to correlate   the astigmatic flowers
   with their perennial names,

I crouch

watch   stretch

                    and disappear

                through the unobserved,

                                uncreated

                                            gates

gargoyle villanelle

How long can he hang here, are they drawing lots?
Someone must have told him what was being gambled,
A long time ago; he's forgotten what it was.

Summer is a dry barrel of thirst.
His soul becomes a birdlimed canker.
How long can he hang here, are they drawing lots?

Others are wilting. Most of the saints have lost
A wing, a key, a halo or an eyeball —
A long time ago; they've forgotten what it was.

Winter, and the angels are stiffening with frost.
He watches geese fly over in an acrobatic gaggle:
How long can he hang here, are they drawing lots?

He heard a rumour once of a camel or an ox.
Or was it just a wrangle over an apple?
A long time ago; he's forgotten what it was.

When will it be his turn to be the Christ?
Pilate asking *What is truth*; Barabbas, released to the rabble?
How long can he hang here? It seems the lots were drawn
A long time ago . . . He's forgotten what his was.

Jesus in the Nursing Home

(i)

If he could remember his address
(it will come to him in a minute)
he could go visit his budgie. He fumbles
for the walker by the bed, steers himself
to the door — yesterday the way
got tangled in his cardigan.
Doors hid their faces. What was
the word for cold? Someone
has shuffled the pack of stars.

Jesus tucks the crocheted quilt tight
around his thighs. Far away down the hall
he can hear the whoosh of someone
vacuuming the lounge. There's nothing
wrong with his ears, but someone
has wiped his eyes
with a bleary sponge. He tries to say
Home, or *What is the time*; the words
come clotted
as the throaty coo of pigeons
walking blurred along the window ledge.

Someone has suffered the rack of stars.
Someone has sewn a cat
into an elastic band. It must be

something to do with why the moon has shrunk
into the mewling
contracts of his heart.

(ii)

Everyone else is sleeping through Gethsemane.
Light shines on a row of pinned faces,
each door marked with photograph and name,
Miss Lorimer, Mr. Watson . . . to infinity.
What name rings tinnitus? Pretty sure
his name is Mr. Watson. This way
always led to his armchair and budgie.
In all the shuffle of stars, he can't find
where they've hidden the wind.

It must be time to go home now. Is it left
or right to the elevator and the goldfish tank?
When (the moon is clamped to the marrow
of his bones) he gets to the goldfish tank
he knows the fish will shine. Surely
it was somewhere
along here, past the table and the tall
vase of flowers. He splashes through
pools of children, mountains and valleys, trying
to find the way back to his room. A face
hovers over him: *How are you this beautiful
sunshiny day?*

      PpppPaa,

he says, *Ppppp Aaaa*
and the angels, darkening, vanish —-

(iii)

The TV isn't on, after all.
The chairs are empty in the lounge.
A dead wasp on the windowsill
crinkles under his finger; hallowed
be thy name. Is it time to go home?
Someone has muffled the clock of stars.

What has become of his address? Which
button should he press to make the elevator
come? He left his name in the alcove
by the bench. He'd better go
find it. What time? It must be
shame to go home now. Which button
should he press — the word for *hold* is
shaky — there's nothing to be
                    ash aaame
            whooch
                    button
should he piss to make
            the elevator

(iv)

Surely this is
the way into the garden.

Now all he has to do is feed the ducks, remember
to take   he'll know
where
he is, what he must
                    bread for the ducks.

(v)

Someone has mocked the ducks; should he
leave them alone to weep? Or maybe
he'll take them into the arms
of his stained beige cardigan
     holy holy holy
pleated in the folds of their wings.

(vi)

He has nothing left to do except forgive:

Carefully, so it doesn't
slip, he holds up the cataracted globe:
the corridor extends
as far as he can see, Miss Lorimer, Mr. Watson,

valley and hill and mountain, river and sands, the woman
he hears vacuuming down the hall, dried wasp
on the windowsill, torturer in East Timor, the man
driving down the street in a yellow Datsun, Moses,
Inge, Ali, Oshowetok, Safia Bibi,

      P a, he says, *PppppP aaa*

all this he must hold, making the snow
fall forever upside down, over
        the word.

Born in northern England, Barbara Colebrook Peace came to
Canada as a student and chose to stay, making this country her
home. Having completed a master's degree in Classical Literature,
she worked for sixteen years as an art gallery manager. She is
currently a poet, reviewer and freelance editor. Her poetry has
been published in literary journals, in her chapbook *Twelve Silences*
(Reference West, 1998), and in the anthologies *Threshold* (Sono
Nis Press, 1998) and *Breaking the Surface* (Sono Nis Press, 2000).
She lives with her husband, Terry Peace, in Victoria, B.C.